The Doors of the Body

The Doors of the Body

Poems by Mary Alexandra Agner

Mayapple Press 2009

Published by   MAYAPPLE PRESS
                   408 N. Lincoln St.
                   Bay City, MI 48708
                   www.mayapplepress.com

ISBN 978-0932412-79-9

ACKNOWLEDGMENTS

Autumn Sky Poetry, The Shield of Thetis; *Barefoot Muse*, Ellen in Egypt; *Blue Mesa Review*, Corn Field, Salem; *Boxcar Poetry Review*, Mercedes; *Crab Creek Review*, Terms (as "Have You Come to Parley?"); *Goblin Fruit*, Wear the Lightning; GROWLING SOFTLY, Troll; *Iron Horse Literary Review*, Yarns; *Naugatuck River Review*, Oh My Darling; *Poemeleon*, Minerva; *Strange Horizons*, Sweets and Sleeping Beauty.

Cover art by Tanakawho. Cover design by Judith Kerman. Book designed and typeset by Amee Schmidt with book titles in QT Antique Post, and poem titles and text in Californian FB.

Contents

The Doors of the Body   3

Ellen in Egypt   4

Sleeping Beauty   5

Wit   6

Old Enough   8

Swan Sonnenizio   9

Oh My Darling   10

Yarns   12

Mercedes   13

Sweets   14

Unhappy in Her Body   16

Like Father, Like Son   17

Wear the Lightning   18

Minerva   20

Growing Up in Thebes   21

Troll   22

Terms   24

Queen Tomyris on the Battlefield   25

The Shield of Thetis   26

The Harvest I Desire   27

Corn Field, Salem   28

Even the Universe Has a Heart   29

The Doors of the Body

Take off your crown, golden tress
which has made light for all your darkness,
and leave it on the murky floor.
You may pass through the first door.

Pull the metal from out your flesh,
wires wound through ears in pain and jest,
and leave them on the chilly floor.
You may pass through the second door.

Count the cobalt neck-beads from off their string,
each year whipped loose, a white wasp's sting,
and lay them, quiet, on the floor.
Enter through the third door.

Scrape bone to bone above your heart,
your cloak of skin will spread apart,
the pin which held it tinkling to the floor.
Make your way through the fourth door.

Reach deep within your mothering womb
for the two white crystals whose brightness croons
as you rock them gently to the floor.
Enter through the fifth door.

Shake off your hands, shake off your feet,
neither lover to warm nor friend to meet
here on the packed earth floor.
Make your way through the sixth door.

Peel off your skin, bend back your bones,
escape from all else but your own
feathers floating above the floor.
You may pass through the seventh door

to the underworld and your sister-self,
jealous, grasping for all your wealth:
no tongue, no throat, but a thirst for more
than can be locked behind any door.

Ellen in Egypt

I had to change my name and cut my hair.
The golden curlicues that spun and dropped
down to the floor, I didn't mind. The sounds
I miss. Husky H. Honeyed. Heady.
Sexy. I could hear it underneath
their need, inaudible as breathing. Lost
like ephithets: daughter of Zeus, the twin
sister of Clytemnestra. The memories
gone too, no more crowded marketplace,
Cly at my side, swaying our hips in time,
our smiles indications of the giggles
pressing to come out. She noticed long
before I did: the avid looks from men
in armor, bloodied, who only spoke of war.
I was still singing to myself, in time
to salsa rhythms beating through my body.
The suitors came. Stern, serious, stiff.
And I was ready for a dance, a whirl
around the floor, skirts spinning out, to show
my ankles off. They chose a man for me
whose steps were full of grace, whose legs were lean.
Instead, he gave up dancing when we wed.
I did not, my skirts were still slit high,
my legs and arms remembered all the moves
even years later, when Paris came,
the soundless H unvoiced under his gasps
for air. In Troy, while battle raged, they banned
all kinds of fun. Achilles promised me
in Egypt we could dance and so I left
with him. Moonlit Nile nights, cats
underfoot, until I lay him down,
fine feet still, after one last dip.

Sleeping Beauty

I was laughing when I died,
picturing the face some future prince
might make when, having hacked
through giant rosebush thorns
and climbed the haunted tower,
he sees the spindle broken and the bed
unmade. We ran out at the last,
my virgin blood still wet between my thighs.
Let the spurned witch-sister
and the so-called fairy godmothers
duke out what history is writ.
Poor planning lets fate devour
the happy story here-and-now.
Destiny wants purity and light
and most of all submission, so
the scullery maid fisted me to ecstasy.
The curse broke like the chiming of a clock.
Time to grow up, unconcerned
by princess pink and bridal white. My passion
saved my life: city, apothecary's shop,
both a husband and a wife,
and grandchildren, bored, about my deathbed—
I would not have waited for a single man,
no matter what his charms,
for what I made with my two hands.

Wit

*And that was how a great scandal threatened to affect the kingdom of
Bohemia, and how the best plans of Mr. Sherlock Holmes were beaten
by a woman's wit.*   —*Arthur Conan Doyle*

Holmes, they have us in bed together.
As if I'd touch you, as if I touched you
even in those frightful moments when I feared
you had been injured for my sake.
It never was your body that I lusted for.

Norton, emperor of my romance,
comfortable weight against my back—
he and I have always been a team.
There is not one regret dropped here
among the pillows and the well-used sheets

but I do miss the frisson between peers.
Would you play the game again?
Or, voice no longer sweet contralto,
breasts no longer prim, can I not beat
into your blood better than cocaine?

Although you eschewed the violence
of feelings that make man man,
is that not what brought you forth:
the hot touch of someone else's intellect?
If it was the body and not the brain

that roused you: I name you hypocrite.
If you would put my cunning and resource
and nerves of steel into a small box
built of letters: Woman plus Intelligence
equals Tragedy, I'll say that William

did it better by two hundred years
and sic the merry wives of Windsor on you.
Tell me biology was not the matter. Tell me,
greatest detective who might have lived—
impossible eliminated—that you deduced

improbable equality as truth.

Old Enough

Old enough to have no name to mark what things she made.
The beautiful words come down through time, but not the maker.

One thousand nights, one thousand loves, and one beautiful name
unlike the wife who wished *blow, western wind*, and died, unmarked
maker.

The gravestones carry dates and names but not the pioneer music
once sung by the marriage-maker, garden-maker, child-maker.

Even great great great grandmother's name fades into silence
although she was the balance-sun-and-rain chant maker.

Tying sayings up like string, rhymes of advice still practical,
sense so common, on all lips, attributed to no one maker and every
maker.

A horse and a reed whistle and a vast continent are not disaster.
Eighteen verses of silk and loneliness outlast their maker.

Always so many more unnamed, unmarked, and in their absence,
perhaps unmade.
Anonymous, prime your pens and prick your needles. Name your-
selves makers.

Swan Sonnenizio

Did she put on his knowledge with his power?
Isn't that what made them shudder, Yeats
and Zeus, that sperm escapes the fates of men

and chooses recombining with the wider world
(and womb) in that white rush? Mastered
by their blood, they become brutes.

Trap her in a tower, burn her, she'll drop
herself out of the flames, unfurl the wings
built from her transformed desperation. Helpless,

they'll watch her dress caught up in air, billowing
to break her fall. Grounded, she will caress
her arms and thighs and make sure she is whole.

Mother by rape, she menaces with claws and beak.
One sudden blow may make her bend, but never break.

Oh My Darling

In my dreams she still doth haunt me,
Robed in garments soaked in brine

I never liked the ducks.
To you they meant good sex, a happy nest,
some safety you had never found
in canyons or in caverns. Or in my own
night-black pit, its beauty why you married me.
I was so sure, as mistress, with husband,
the ducks would stay to keep my father company.
And yet you asked for them as dowry!
You laughed as though your sides
might cave in when you watched me
drive them home. Your scrunched-up skin
made me forget the dashing gent
whose arms divided culture and backwater,
who quoted poetry, who promised one more rush
and we'd be rich enough to leave.

Not so difficult to guess that I was day-dreaming
while wading with the ducks: droppings, fewmets,
fundamentally lousy birds. I fell—
one too many webbed flat feet entwining mine.
There was no splinter.
When I hit the cold, I welcomed how unavian
the water's roaring was, not loud enough
to drown your laughter while I drowned.

Oh, darling, they were still chording "Clementine"
when you turned out the ducks and bedded down
with my best friend. She took you
to my funeral. I did my Ophelia-best:
bloated, floating, flowers strewn, stems
poking my eyelids, opening them.
I stood up from the shallows. The whole town watched
my body pass, instead of me, upright and grinning.

Tonight, your new wife out, I hover
between you and the window. Your nostrils twitch.
The smell of cold water death catches you
in sneezes. The moonlight makes me visible.
I reach out my arms, shuffle my feet—
duck feathers still cling to my ghostly skin—
and stroke your throat. I would give anything
to strangle you, but that would let you in
this poultry-empty place. Instead, I let go
of your bones and skin and air and wait.
When consciousness crawls back inside your eyes
I am the first thing you will see.

Yarns

Gone two decades, almost ghost
in my memory, I recognize right
away the hitch in your voice, inhaling
for time to find the perfect
lie. You're home for good.
This close, I smell all the traveling
years caught in your clothes,
the mix of man's bloody war,
the perfect godly perfume
of Athena's touch, the touch of Nausikaa,
the sea salt dried like diamonds.
It doesn't take a sorceress to hide
the truth with art. Old age
awakens many powers in the eyes
and ears of married women.
I've warmed the bed. Tonight at least
you'll curl into the S-shape of my heat.

I've listened to your tales. Abuse
of words always was your greatest fault,
your greatest talent. What irony,
that Tennyson would twist your story,
bully you onto a ship, all the oceans,
steal you from my small embrace
with words that crowd out any kiss
from me that is not *goodbye*,
a promise to keep chaste,
to wait, whittled, the way clouds
of wool become taut strands
snarled into a knot of hate.

Mercedes

What made you think that I had stayed in stasis
for the fourteen years you were in prison?
You would have been the first to throw a stone:
witch, unnatural, if I had waited, patient,
penniless, imprisoned by my memory of you—
instead of doing as the culture and our times dictated.
Marriage to a rich man made my days as empty
as a fishing net picked over onland for tears.
When I gave birth to Albert, I spoke three languages
besides my Catalan and your Français; I kept the house
accounts and caught the steward as he siphoned off
the funds he thought my husband would not miss;
I painted landscapes, sketched a face;
my idle hands have wrung the soul out of the spinet.
And you: no more a naive sailor.
I think we'd suit, in our old age.

Sophistication sloughs off as you speak.
I wince from your demands.
When I say "leave" and you hear "let me be alone
within my misery," I mean, "when you have gone,
so goes my obligation to the past;
all the rooms that I have built will fling
their doors wide open to the brine, the night sky,
to the singular and many-faceted epiphany
that I have made more of myself
than all your daydreams of me ever did."

Sweets

I hear the argument outside the house
each time my grandchildren arrive:
must we smile, *must* we thank her
even though she never gives us sweets?

Even great-uncle Hansel gives them cake
and cookies. At home, they eat desserts
and candied snacks, begin to whisper
I am the witch and not the victim

from the news, the not-quite-scary bedtime story.
They think I cannot bear to have sweets
in the house, but all these years,
I've shown restraint.

My brother, fast-asleep, homesick and weary,
naive and blessed, never tasted that house
at sunrise: sugar stucco, caramel latch
that melted as I lifted it, dripping.

He snored. The witch gave me a spoonful
of pudding, exquisite, unlike anything
I've ever known. The hard sweetness
still burned my throat as she explained

the recipe, the flesh of youth cooked down,
and I must swallow, or choke. Ready disciple,
I learned I was a coward: too timid to push
my brother into the fire, too afraid to pull

the witch out when she fell.
Sweets still have their special taste:
gasoline, sometimes chalk. Vidalias
can get to be too much in allium season.

Still arguing, the children knock
and enter. Quite soon, their parents
will leave them here, alone with me,
the way my husband never let *them* be.

In my hunger, my lifetime abstinence,
I have long understood the frosting of deceit,
the ease with which one can believe
anything of gumdrops.

Unhappy in Her Body

Pigs! They said I turned them into swine?
I wanted company. A girl must have
her gossip, a woman wants the extra
pair of hands for work and play.
My island was a lonely place;
ignorant of how much of an extrovert
I was, I'd left the world behind.
And now, I hear their version of the story:
snuffling, sties, and daily mud baths,
when in truth I gave them breasts and menses
and the ability to float out in the ocean.
Cat fights resolved with kisses.
I loved them all, made love to them all,
missed not one bit their beards or balls.

Everyone on down the line knew.
The sirens nagged, the best bitches in history,
Charybdis pulled them toward her clit,
Scylla did six men at once.
They made them squeal as the hogs they wished to be.

Why let them go? No woman
should be as unhappy in her body
as he was. And also, his wife:
she deserved what years were left in him.

Like Father, Like Son

You thought Athena came to you, disguised
as one you trusted. Afterwards, of course.
At the time, there was just the old friend
of your father's, not often seen, unexpected
but so welcome with his advice
that got you off of Ithaka, cold rock,
away from all parental oversight
and aided you in finding out
your father's whereabouts.
It was a woman, yes, who came to you,
who put on man's tunic, removed her makeup
to bring out her golden, calloused skin,
who rigged the lines and sailed the boat,
who spoke with you of just what duty is.

You thought Athena came to you, disguised
you as a swineherd, all the better
to display your wily feats of mind
to the suitors and the daily lives of Ithaka.
The dog knew who you were.
But after twenty years—even had you boasted
of me as a goddess when newly-married—
you could not recognize your wife
although my face was bare, hair in helm.
You spent our conversation looking at the ground.
In twenty years I'd passed as sailor
many times, to Troy and back.
I even armed you once, before a battle.
I knew you were alive. I kept you
that way, because I know what duty is.

Wear the Lightning

The Goddess of Death sent servants
bearing gifts: the water-gift, the grain-gift,
everything a hostess might require
of a guest, and I refused them everything.

They threatened me with thunder,
they threatened me with rain,
they made the earth move and I fell.
And I refused them everything.

Like men intent on brutal sex
they tore my clothes and spread me wide.
They poured the lightning straight into my womb
and I refused them everything.

Brother, they have come and searched and gone,
convinced no sister would yield up
what would betray the brother
who never refused her anything.

Inanna, brightness of Heaven,
I do not begrudge you either of your sons.
I do what I must to save my brother.
Grant me one gift, who has never refused you anything:

give me half my brother's fate,
take me to the place my brother lies,
take me to the place your husband lies.
I wear the lightning. Refuse me anything

and I will bring out from my womb
the blackened heat, I will bring forth
mudmen with bloodshot eyes, I will birth in you
the pain felt by the one whom you refused everything:

Dumuzi, shepherd, lover, husband, brother,
sacrifice to your own skin and power,
who died in love and in confusion,
who never refused you anything.

Minerva

Sprung fully formed, they say, the spitting image
with spear for stand-in phallus and an owlet
to hold my wisdom, since my little female
noggin couldn't hold the liquid measure
itself, of course. The model for Pygmalion.
No childhood. No teenage angst to foment
rebellion toward my elders, the dish only
a man would serve his father with. An action
figurine with blunted blade and buxom
behind and hips. No mother and no sisters.

Father, you never asked if I had longings
exceeding your narrow-minded need for power.
Indeed, you never knew that I was more than
another arm until you sought persuasion—
the kind that women work—as part of warring.
But I am more than limb or lips or message
delivery girl when I take nymph or man
into my bed. I've found a strength, not anger
or intellect; to share without surrender.
I have stepped out from under your long shadow.

Growing Up in Thebes

I have seen sundown linger,
blizzards silence
what daylight winter offers,
all the endings
by which nature puts out light,
even the stars.
You shuffle in a greater darkness,
man-made, hand-made.

Father, your grip hurts
as I let you go
past the postern, old but hale
and blind.
I do not care what rash acts
brought you here.
I can see your eyes slide past me.
I have spent so much
of my life crying, "Look, Daddy, look
at me!"

Troll

Listening to the river I stop listening
for your footsteps coming after me.
I watch the fish dart, terrified and hopeful
someday I could be as quick
to slip between harm's fingers.
The bruises on my hands have faded,
but my skin's now blue and stiff;
my fingers do not meet my palms
except the pointed nails, which I found new
this morning. The day before, you caned my legs
when I mistook the sugar for the salt,
and yesterday I felt bone ridges rising
from the lines; today they're two-inch spikes.
To keep boys from the wrong idea, you shaped
and kneaded head and hair by hand.
The taste of blood eclipsed my mouth,
red cauldron which rebirthed my teeth
as fangs. The boxing echoed in my mind,
each repetition lengthening my ears to flaps.
I look terrible. And terrifying.

I feel the tremor of your shoes against
the ground, this arch which spans the water.
Do you even see me anymore
or just the lazy slut who won't transform
into a perfect baker's daughter? You stop.
I stand up; I look down at you.
Small man, today I've seen the self
you've made of me. I choose to wear
your mask of beatings and betrayals.
This is my bridge.
I will take a toll from you, to cross it.
I will take a toll from you for each time you crossed
that line and battered me. Let me show you
my new claws, dig them in your flour-white skin.

Just how much of your torso fits between my jaws?
Oh, I will grind your bones down
and suck the sweetness from your flesh,
until no memory of fame for pie or cake remains.

Terms

Oh, proud Kleomenes, king of Sparta, powerful men
of Sparta, with your gleaming shields, chosen
for your ruthlessness and prowess,
I, Telesilla of Argos, writer of songs, address
you and your muscled hands prepared to rend,
to crush our bronze thighs. Women ascend
our walls, there, over the gates, spears near
to hand. Did you expect a trembling fear?
Or door and jamb parted like our loose hair
because our men are gone? Instead, we wear
rough armor, take up bucklers, fill the boiling pots
with oil and water. This is the bloody spot
where you will die at the hands of Argive women,
your skulls cracked, your ribs bent in
to pierce your hearts, your faces burnt away.
Now, have you come for parley?

Queen Tomyris on the Battlefield

It did not matter that *they* had pinned Cyrus
the Great—my strong-armed steppe barbarians,
men the age of my son, men who would live
long past this day which my son would not—

pinned him to the ground, a man for each quarter—
Cyrus, King of the World's Four Rims—a man kneeling
into the center of his back, as he struggled, captured,
like my captured son had surged and fought.

I was the one—small sword,
hilt thin enough for the slim fingers of a boy—
who looked last into his eyes, saw the cloud-sky
color the people said *his* son inherited,

I who stomped his face into the dirt,
hefted the blade over my head as axe,
and let it fall like the setting sun
through skin and soul and on into the soil.

The Shield of Thetis

I should have finished what I started.
Nine months and the immortal blood
I passed to him were not enough
to keep him from his human destiny.

So much of that was self-fulfilling:
what teenage boy avoids the surge
of war that mimics how his power rises,
new, from childish limbs to hairy legs?

I sought the metalsmith, but his was iron
bent instead of bled and in the end
I know the body, bones and ligaments, the best.
Thigh for armpiece, rib for crossbar,
my longest hairs to hold my skin stretched taut.

If only I were proud of all his slaughter,
proud that he fit all his wallowing grief
to a cause his world considered just:
that girls should not be raped, nor boys
allowed to knife each other without rules.

He did not ask for prophecy,
but neither did he learn the body
bent and broken never ends revenge
and never purges sadness.
                                  Neither did I.

The Harvest I Desire

after apple-picking

The orchard's empty, though the rain has stopped.
Out here among the Jonagolds, Macouns,
a thousand thousand names for fruit,
we are alone.
At first I thought you'd dropped
the apple, bitten to the white,
in favor of those trapped at ladder-height.
Instead, you need two hands to hold mine tight.
You kiss me with such urgency
I know that from this tree
I too can take the harvest I desire.
You push me up against the bark
so its tough fingers scar
my back, the ache as tree leans down on me
as we lean into it will leave its mark
in nine month's time.
                                I know my ancestors—
the wicked stepmother still plots, and Eve
has seen this fall before—
but to me an apple is an apple:
core, seeds, blossoms the wind will scatter far,
and cider made to ward off year-end chill.
I have plucked a child from the stillness
of dying leaves. I shall exult
and set the wet autumnal sky afire.

Corn Field, Salem

This is the fruit that would grow from my body
were I burned at the stake and that stake forgotten:
a farmer's crooked furrows, green breaking the ground
with the hair of a comet, then bursting through husks,
still alive and ripe-blushing, to meet with the earth.

And the pattern of kernels, the Morse code that taps
out the next of my lives: purpled and spiraled,
a rod in the hand of the minister preaching
the long warmth and light to those who believe
and thumping the corn on his Good Book for thunder.

My body is maize, blaze far in the future,
now ankles aflame with runner bean scratches,
my toes dug in dirt, as I drop down the seed,
wrinkled white kernels. On the horizons, the drought
of adulthood, the sweet singing voice from inside the pyre.

Even the Universe Has a Heart

pumping, pushing blood from the center
out to each edge, each individual,
be she jaguar, gypsy, junco, cactus,
off-kilter caterwauling child crazy
with the first flush of fall cooling the *cenote*.
But that heart is a sieve, something the gods
made to be filled, to mark the pact
between creator and created, and it slurps
the sweet liquid as it soaks into the stone,
the salty liquid into the stone,
and the stone soaks into the earth
and the earth emerges into the realm of the gods.
Sweet and precious, we honor the blood,
we honor the gods, we uphold the heart
of the world by carrying it within our bodies.
In death, in blood spilled out
in daily piercings to keep the world alive,
our loved ones alive, the quetzalcoatl alive,
we honor the heart of the world.
Why would I withhold my life
for the life of the universe?
My last sunrise pounds knives of light
into my skin and my eyes, final vision
of the City from the heights, feathers flush
against my arms, my breasts,
my ankles and calves, dipped blue in the sacred
bird, fanned out, then stripped,
chicken-skinned, the flesh willing,
as the priest brings down the knife, singing.

About the Author

Mary Alexandra Agner writes of dead women, telescopes, and secrets. She was born in a United State made for lovers and currently lives outside Boston. Her family tree bears Parson Brown oranges. Her advanced degrees include Earth and planetary science, and creative writing; she's blessed to have a paying job that utilizes both of them. All her life she's observed the universe and written about it. She can be found online at *http://www.pantoum.org/*.

Other Recent Titles from Mayapple Press:

Rhoda Stamell, *The Art of Ruin*, 2009
      Paper, 126 pp, $16.95 plus s&h
      ISBN 978-0932412-782
Marion Boyer, *The Clock of the Long Now*, 2009
      Paper, 88 pp, $15.95 plus s&h
      ISBN 978-0932412-775
Tim Mayo, *The Kingdom of Possibilities*, 2009
      Paper, 78 pp, $14.95 plus s&h
      ISBN 978-0932412-768
Allison Joseph, *Voice: Poems*, 2009
      Paper, 36 pp, $12.95 plus s&h
      ISBN 978-0932412-751
Josie Kearns, *The Theory of Everything*, 2009
      Paper, 86 pp, $14.95 plus s&h
      ISBN 978-0932412-744
Eleanor Lerman, *The Blonde on the Train*, 2009
      Paper, 164 pp, $16.95 plus s&h
      ISBN 978-0932412-737
Sophia Rivkin, *The Valise*, 2008
      Paper, 38 pp, $12.95 plus s&h
      ISBN 978-0932412-720
Alice George, *This Must Be the Place*, 2008
      Paper, 48 pp, $12.95 plus s&h
      ISBN 978-0932412-713
Angela Williams, *Live from the Tiki Lounge*, 2008
      Paper, 48 pp, $12.95 plus s&h
      ISBN 978-0932412-706
Claire Keyes, *The Question of Rapture*, 2008
      Paper, 72 pp, $14.95 plus s&h
      ISBN 978-0932412-690
Judith Kerman and Amee Schmidt, eds., *Greenhouse: The First 5 Years of the Rustbelt Roethke Writers' Workshop*, 2008
      Paper, 78 pp, $14.95 plus s&h
      ISBN 978-0932412-683
Cati Porter, *Seven Floors Up*, 2008
      Paper, 66 pp, $14.95 plus s&h
      ISBN 978-0932412-676
Rabbi Manes Kogan, *Fables from the Jewish Tradition*, 2008
      Paper, 104 pp, $19.95 plus s&h
      ISBN 978-0932412-669

For a complete catalog of Mayapple Press publications, please visit our website at *www.mayapplepress.com*. Books can be ordered direct from our website with secure on-line payment using PayPal, or by mail (check or money order). Or order through your local bookseller.